CodeStar Connection
Management Woes

Table of Contents

1. Introduction 1

2. Demystifying CodeStar Connection Management 2

    2.1. Understanding CodeStar Connection Management 2

    2.2. Creating a Connection in AWS CodeStar 3

    2.3. Connection States in AWS CodeStar 3

    2.4. The Challenge of Token Rotation 4

    2.5. Interacting with Connection API Operations 4

    2.6. Connection Management Best Practices 5

3. Understanding the Core Components 6

    3.1. AWS CodeStar 6

    3.2. Project Dashboard 6

    3.3. AWS CodeCommit 7

    3.4. AWS CodeBuild 7

    3.5. AWS CodeDeploy 7

    3.6. AWS CodePipeline 7

    3.7. AWS Elastic Beanstalk 8

    3.8. IAM in AWS CodeStar 8

    3.9. Amazon S3 8

    3.10. Amazon CloudWatch 8

    3.11. AWS Lambda 8

4. Common Connection Issues and Their Triggers 10

    4.1. Issue 1: Project Creation Failures 10

    4.2. Issue 2: Connection Timeouts 10

    4.3. Issue 3: Pipeline Execution Hangs 11

    4.4. Issue 4: VPC Connectivity Errors 11

5. Architectural Drawbacks and Their Impact 13

    5.1. Microservice Dependencies 13

    5.2. Self-Contained Systems 14

5.3. Data Consistency in Distributed Systems 14

5.4. Serverless Architectures 15

6. Establishing an Efficient Connection: A Step-by-Step Guide 16

6.1. Understanding Required Components 16

6.2. Setting up IAM roles 16

6.3. Creating a CodeStar Project 17

6.4. Setting up CodePipeline 17

6.5. Establishing the Connection 18

6.6. Conclusion 18

7. The Role of Network Configuration in Connection Stability 20

7.1. Understanding Network Configuration 20

7.2. The Network Blueprint 20

7.3. Getting the VPCs Right 21

7.4. Finessing Subnets 22

7.5. Deciphering Routing Tables and Internet Gateways 22

8. Diagnosing and Fixing Connection Woes 24

8.1. Understanding Connection Flow 24

8.2. Diagnosing Connection Problems 25

8.2.1. Error Messages 25

8.2.2. Log Files 25

8.3. Fixing Connection Problems 26

8.3.1. Adjusting User Permissions 26

8.3.2. Verifying Resource Availability 26

8.3.3. Correcting Request Structure 26

8.4. The Ping Test 26

8.5. Securing Your Connection 27

9. Productive Troubleshooting Tools and Techniques 28

9.1. Understanding Comprehensively 28

9.2. Using the AWS Management Console 29

9.3. AWS CLI and SDKs 29

9.4. Using AWS CloudWatch 30

9.5. Integrating with AWS X-Ray 30

9.6. Expert Tip: AWS Trusted Advisor 30

10. Best Practices in CodeStar Connection Management 32

10.1. Understanding Connection Management 32

10.2. Setting Up CodeStar Connections 33

10.3. Implementing Connection Security 33

10.4. Troubleshooting Connection Issues 34

11. Looking Ahead: The Future of CodeStar and Connection

Management 36

11.1. The Advent of Automated Connection Management 36

11.2. The Role of AI in Connection Management 37

11.3. Enhancing the User Experience with Interactive

Interfaces 37

11.4. Fortifying Security in Connection Management 37

11.5. Integration with More AWS Services 38

11.6. Conclusion 38

Chapter 1. Introduction

The age-old adage, "No tool is perfect," proves true once again in our latest Special Report on 'CodeStar Connection Management Woes'. Even the most seasoned developers often find themselves stumped while navigating the fascinating yet complex world of AWS CodeStar, as they wrangle with its connection management intricacies. This detailed report will be your comprehensive guide - stripping back the layers of mystique and giving you a practical, hands-on approach to tackle any connectivity issue that CodeStar could toss your way. Whether you're an aspiring cloud developer or an experienced DevOps mastermind, you'll discover eye-opening insights and solutions within the pages of our report that may turn your CodeStar frown upside down. With an easy-to-understand, down-to-earth format, we hope to make this highly technical topic accessible and engaging to all our readers. Every hurdle can be a stepping stone to greater knowledge - let us lead the way with this robust report!

Chapter 2. Demystifying CodeStar Connection Management

First of all, we must grasp the fundamentals of AWS CodeStar, starting from the very beginning and afterwards moving on to a higher level of intricacy. CodeStar is an AWS service designed to strengthen teams' application development capabilities by offering an integrated environment for collaboration and agile project management.

One of the pivotal features of AWS CodeStar is its connection management, which allows resource-based authorization of connections from third-party source providers, thereby providing a safeguard for your AWS resources. Here we delve deeper into this critical functionality offered by AWS CodeStar.

2.1. Understanding CodeStar Connection Management

CodeStar connection management is not a standalone service, but a feature integrated into the CodeStar structure. It helps developers to streamline DevOps activities by facilitating smoothly maintained connections to third-party code repositories.

In essence, CodeStar uses AWS Secrets Manager secrets and AWS Security Token Service (STS) to securely host connection ARNs (Amazon Resource Name) and associated third-party access tokens. These tokens participate in critical functions, including -

1. Capturing and storing connection details

2. Resources authorization

3. Token rotation

2.2. Creating a Connection in AWS CodeStar

For interaction with a third-party provider, CodeStar creates and manages 'connections'. A connection is essentially a gateway through which AWS services interact with external agencies. When you set up a connection, you're asked to provide access to a third-party source provider such as GitHub.

To do so, follow these steps:

1. Open the AWS Management Console.
2. Navigate to 'AWS CodeStar' > 'Connections'.
3. Click on 'Create Connection'.
4. Provide the necessary permissions and authorizations for the third-party source that you're connecting.
5. Save the details – and voila, your connection is created.

2.3. Connection States in AWS CodeStar

Connections in AWS CodeStar have different states that indicate the status of third-party affiliations. There are primarily four connection states:

1. 'PENDING' when a connection has been created but is not yet functional.
2. 'AVAILABLE' when a connection has been used successfully at least once and is ready for further use.

3. 'UNAVAILABLE' when a connection is long unused or disabled by AWS due to prolonged inactivity.

4. 'Deleted' when a connection has been intentionally removed by the user.

2.4. The Challenge of Token Rotation

One of the main stumbling blocks experienced in CodeStar connections is token rotation. CodeStar uses OAuth tokens, received from third-party source providers, in order to maintain connections with these providers. However, these tokens are not everlasting; they periodically expire, requiring a token rotation process.

While the token rotation can be a complex matter, it is crucial in maintaining a secure connection and is a part of smart access management. The AWS Secrets Manager service assists in rotating these tokens.

2.5. Interacting with Connection API Operations

AWS CodeStar connections offer APIs that simplify interaction with different features. These APIs provide methods for creating, listing, and deleting connections. They also enable users to get connection details, update connections, and retrieve metadata.

The most important part here is understanding the specific operations. Each one has a unique role and requirement. The table below explains the primary API operations:

|Operation |Description | |---------------|---------------| |CreateConnection|Creates a connection to a third-party source provider.| |GetConnection |Fetches metadata and status of a connection.| |ListConnections |Lists all available connections.|

|UpdateConnection|Updates an existing connection instance.|
|DeleteConnection|Deletes a specified connection.|

2.6. Connection Management Best Practices

Put forth are a few tried and true best practices for managing CodeStar connections:

1. **Establish a clean access control system:** Implement proper access controls to restrict who can create, alter, use, or delete connections.

2. **Token rotation maintenance:** Ensure timely token rotations for maintaining healthy, secure connections.

3. **Balanced utilization:** Maintain an appropriate number of connections to avoid clutter and manage resources effectively.

4. **Utilize APIs efficiently:** Maximize benefits from connection API operations to automate and streamline your tasks.

In summary, connection management is one of the key aspects of using AWS CodeStar effectively and securely. As you appreciate and understand its utility, your CodeStar experience will inevitably become smoother and more productive. As we wrap up this section, we leave you with an assurance that the next time you deal with connections in CodeStar; it will be a less daunting and more enriching experience.

In the forthcoming chapters, we will explore more on various facets of AWS CodeStar that are critical to catapult you into DevOps stardom. Stay with us to unravel the next layer of mysteries.

Chapter 3. Understanding the Core Components

Before we dive into the complexities of managing connections in AWS CodeStar, developing an in-depth understanding of the core components involved is key. This will not only pinpoint where connectivity issues typically originate but also how to serve and mitigate them effectively.

Let's take a deep dive into the key components of AWS CodeStar, untangling it knot by knot for a better grasp of its workings.

3.1. AWS CodeStar

AWS CodeStar is an integrated development service designed to streamline the process of quickly developing, building, and deploying applications on AWS. It is primarily designed to aid users in developing, building, and deploying applications on AWS, all with the viability of choosing their preferred coding language. Its primary components include the project dashboard, AWS CodeCommit, AWS CodeBuild, AWS CodeDeploy, and AWS CodePipeline.

3.2. Project Dashboard

The project dashboard is a centralized location from where you can track and manage all your AWS CodeStar project resources. This includes a continuous delivery toolchain set up, application health and status, and monitoring, including links to committing histories, build results, and deployment activities.

3.3. AWS CodeCommit

Within the scope of AWS CodeStar, AWS CodeCommit is the source control service. It functions as a fully managed source control service that hosts secure Git-based repositories. CodeCommit eliminates the need to operate your source control system while providing a secure, scalable, and cost-effective solution for hosting private Git repositories.

3.4. AWS CodeBuild

AWS CodeBuild is your compiling solution - an entirely managed build service. It compiles your source code, runs unit tests, and produces ready-to-deploy artifacts. CodeBuild scales continuously and processes multiple builds concurrently, which hinders no waiting and fosters productive use of your time.

3.5. AWS CodeDeploy

AWS CodeDeploy takes charge of deploying released code to a fleet of servers, doing so automatically for fast and reliable application updates.

3.6. AWS CodePipeline

AWS CodePipeline personifies your development workflow - an integral part of your work with AWS CodeStar. It's a fully managed Continuous Delivery service that enables you to automate your release pipelines, improving the speed and quality of your application updates.

3.7. AWS Elastic Beanstalk

Outside of CodeStar, another essential to the AWS suite is AWS Elastic Beanstalk. It's an easy-to-use service perfect for deploying and scaling applications developed with Java, .NET, PHP, Node.js, Python, Ruby, Go, and Docker.

3.8. IAM in AWS CodeStar

Identity and Access Management (IAM) play a massive role in AWS CodeStar. This integrated AWS service holds the control to authentication and authorization, essential for secure AWS service interactions. It regulates which users or applications can access which resources - forging security in managing AWS resource access.

3.9. Amazon S3

Amazon S3, with its secure, durable, and highly scalable object storage, plays a crucial role in storing and retrieving any amount of data from anywhere on the web. Here, you can set up the bucket to store your application code and all the necessary resources.

3.10. Amazon CloudWatch

Amazon CloudWatch is essential for your applications running on AWS; it assists you in monitoring through logs and specific metrics accumulated over time. CodeStar integrates with CloudWatch to offer you real-time application insights.

3.11. AWS Lambda

Cloud computing with AWS is incomplete without AWS Lambda, supporting several coding languages and connecting them to other

AWS services. With AWS CodeStar, you can direct your code builds directly onto Lambda, allowing your applications to access the function they need.

Now that we have unwrapped the core components of AWS CodeStar, we have formed a solid foundation. Up next, we'll examine how these components interact to form a cohesive entity in the vast world of AWS, paving the way to proficient connectivity issue management.

Chapter 4. Common Connection Issues and Their Triggers

Connectivity problems with AWS CodeStar can emerge from a variety of sources. They can appear during project creation, when making updates, or even after successful deployment due to changes in the environment. In this chapter, we will dissect several common connection issues and their triggers, along with some potential solutions.

4.1. Issue 1: Project Creation Failures

A frequent case we've observed are issues while creating a project in CodeStar. For example, you might encounter the following error: "AWS CodeStar is unable to create your project. Check the IAM role."

This usually happens due to insufficient permissions in your IAM role. Although AWS CodeStar does automatically attempt to create service roles for IAM during project creation, these can fail if the necessary permissions are not in place.

Solution: It's important that all necessary permissions (like "iam:CreateServiceRole") are granted to your IAM role. After doing so, you should be able to create a project in CodeStar without repeat issues.

4.2. Issue 2: Connection Timeouts

Another familiar issue is that AWS CodeStar services seem to timeout without immediate explanation. This could be due to an extensive number of factors, but some are more prevalent than others.

1. Security group rules

2. Network ACLs (access control lists)

3. Route Table configuration

Solution: In each case, it's essential to scrutinise each potential area for irregularities or oversights. Verify that your security group rules allow for the required access, cross-check network ACLs for any mismatched settings or filters blocking traffic, and make sure your route tables are correctly configured so as not to deny access to any necessary resources.

4.3. Issue 3: Pipeline Execution Hangs

There are situations where AWS CodeStar project's pipeline execution may hang indefinitely without much clarity. This might happen due to the following:

- Timeout during the CodeBuild stage

- Timeout during the CodeDeploy stage

- CodeCommit repository is not accessible

- CodeStar project role does not have the right permissions

Solution: Check for any timeout situations during the CodeBuild and CodeDeploy stages. Adequate access to the CodeCommit repository and the right permissions for CodeStar project role are critical.

4.4. Issue 4: VPC Connectivity Errors

Another common issue lies with VPC (Virtual Private Cloud) connectivity. In cases like these, incorrect VPC configurations or conflicting security group settings can halt connectivity.

Solution: Verify your VPC configuration. Remember to scrutinise your Subnets, Internet Gateways, NAT Gateways, and Security Group rules. Ensure that they are all correctly set up and functioning correctly. You may need to update these settings or engage with AWS Support for help.

In conclusion, while AWS CodeStar is a powerful tool, users may sometimes encounter connectivity hurdles due to a myriad of reasons, such as insufficient IAM roles, connection timeouts due to network complexities, VPC configuration pitfalls and even pipeline execution idiosyncrasies. However, understanding the potential triggers and how to troubleshoot them can make these issues less daunting, helping you to leverage AWS CodeStar effectively.

By approaching each hurdle as an opportunity to learn and grow, you can fill in any knowledge gaps, improve your workflow, and obtain a better handle on CodeStar's connection intricacies. This chapter was designed to shed light on the most common issues and their underlying triggers, as well as provide you with practical solutions. Armed with this knowledge, you should be better equipped to handle any connection management issues you might encounter in AWS CodeStar.

Chapter 5. Architectural Drawbacks and Their Impact

AWS CodeStar, while a powerful tool for streamlined development, is not without its quirks and nuances. In this chapter, we will delve into a few architectual drawbacks that inherently impact AWS CodeStar's connection management capability, alongside ways to navigate these challenges.

Foremost among these architectural limitations is the dependencies between highly coupled microservices. CodeStar Connection management can become increasingly complex and challenging when multiple microservices tightly depend on each other. The failure of one microservice could cause a ripple effect, leading to overall disruption which, in turn, compounds the connection management woes.

5.1. Microservice Dependencies

In a microservices architectural style, developers tend to design the services to be loosely coupled, allowing for greater flexibility and resilience. However, in certain scenarios, as the complexity of the application grows, it can lead to services unintentionally becoming highly coupled. This intensifies the difficulty of managing connections between the services, increases the risk of outage due to a single point failure, and can cause overall system performance degradation.

In these cases, to manage connections more effectively, it's critical to maintain a well-updated service map detailing service interactions. This service map can be easily visualized using tools like AWS X-Ray, which could aid in troubleshooting connection-related issues.

It's also imperative to consider strategies such as circuit breakers to handle any unforeseen failures in a service and prevent the failure from cascading to other interdependent services. AWS CodeStar can integrate with AWS Step Functions to handle such scenarios and ensure that connections are managed more effectively.

5.2. Self-Contained Systems

Another architectural challenge with CodeStar is the encouragement of Self-Contained Systems (SCS) methodology. This approach promotes creating a system consisting of individual, autonomous, and loosely coupled services, each with their own front-end and supporting services, connected together to form the whole system. While a positive choice for robustness and flexibility, this methodology can present a unique set of challenges when it comes to managing connections, especially during cross-communication amongst the SCSs.

To improve the management of connections in SCS-based architecture, it's significant to incorporate robust monitoring, logging, and load balancing services. Applications, like AWS CloudWatch, AWS ELB, and AWS CloudTrail, bring a lot of value in maintaining visibility of connections and informing how they should be managed.

5.3. Data Consistency in Distributed Systems

Distributed systems inherently suffer from consistency issues. As services distributed across different systems try to communicate with each other, a lack of a single, unified source of truth can lead to inconsistency in data. This, invariably, is another connection management challenge to be addressed.

When dealing with distributed systems, it's critical to implement strategies for eventual consistency like Amazon DynamoDB's built-in support for ACID transactions, which guarantees consistent, isolated, and durable transactions to help maintain data integrity across services.

5.4. Serverless Architectures

Serverless architectures emerge as another culprit in the mix, making connection management in CodeStar more difficult. Lack of server management can lead to no control over when and where functions will execute, creating unpredictability in connection management.

In such scenarios, functions within AWS Lambda can be allotted a specific duration and can take care of scaling automatically. AWS Lambda can handle incoming request traffic and monitor function metrics automatically to maintain a steady number of running instances, helping to manage connections more efficiently in a serverless architecture.

In conclusion, while these architectural drawbacks present their own unique challenges, they can be addressed with the right strategies and tools. The path to mastering AWS CodeStar Connection Management might be specked with obstacles, but with a keen eye and a patient approach, there is no difficulty that cannot be overcome.

Understanding these architectural drawbacks and their impacts poses an imperative step in this journey, allowing developers to proactively deal with potential connection woes and streamline their AWS CodeStar experience. As with any tool, there is a learning curve involved, but as we navigate these challenges together, we hope to help you turn these hurdles into stepping stones towards becoming an AWS CodeStar artisan.

Chapter 6. Establishing an Efficient Connection: A Step-by-Step Guide

Let's start by understanding that setting up an efficient connection in AWS CodeStar is not a one tool affair; it's an orchestration of multiple AWS services like CloudFormation, CodePipeline, and many more, working seamlessly to give you a complete DevOps experience. To create this symphony, there are several steps you need to follow.

6.1. Understanding Required Components

Before we start the connection process, it's vital to understand the tools at your disposal. To establish a steady connection, you'll need a good understanding of:

1. Amazon IAM: IAM roles permit AWS services to interact with each other. We require several IAM roles while setting up CodeStar.

2. AWS CloudFormation: It's a service that helps to set up and model AWS resources. In CodeStar, our project is a CloudFormation stack.

3. AWS CodePipeline: We'll use CodePipeline for Continuous Integration/Continuous Deployment (CI/CD).

6.2. Setting up IAM roles

The first step in setting up a connection in CodeStar is to create appropriate IAM roles. Navigate to the IAM console, and follow the steps mentioned below:

1. Create a role with enough permissions to manage your CodeStar project, including full access to CloudFormation and CodePipeline, and underlying resources like CodeCommit, S3, etc. You can name it CodeStarServiceRole.

2. Create another role to be assumed by CodeStar. Call this one CodeStarWorkerRole. This role requires s3:GetObject and s3:GetObjectVersion permissions.

Adopting a meticulous approach in setting up IAM roles can save you from unwanted permission-based errors in the future.

6.3. Creating a CodeStar Project

After setting up the IAM roles, we will now create a CodeStar project.

1. Navigate to the CodeStar console, click on "Create a new Project".

2. Select a template for your project based on the language and the AWS service you wish to use.

3. Next, you'll be asked to name your project, specify the Repository, the Availability Zone, etc. Configure those based on your requirements.

4. Here, you'll have to set the IAM role we created before, AWSCodeStarServiceRole.

5. Finally, review all the details and click "Create Project".

A new CloudFormation Stack, representing your CodeStar project will be in the process of being created.

6.4. Setting up CodePipeline

Now, let's move on to setting up CodePipeline in CodeStar.

1. Navigate to the CodePipeline console.

2. Create a new pipeline and name it. Then, choose CodeStarWorkerRole as the IAM role for this.

3. For the source provider, select AWS CodeStar.

4. Mention the CloudFormation stack name of your CodeStar project as the source.

5. Set up the Build and Deploy Stages based on your need.

6. Review the details and create the Pipeline.

6.5. Establishing the Connection

With all the components in place, it's time we establish the connection.

1. Go back to your CodeStar Project, click on "Connect a tool".

2. You'll find three options: AWS Cloud9, Command Line Tools, and Visual Studio. Select based on your requirements.

3. Follow the steps mentioned by CodeStar to complete the connection process.

Whether you chose AWS Cloud9, Command Line Tools, or Visual Studio will determine if you need to provide different additional information.

Congratulations, your connection is now established, and CodeStar is ready to handle all your DevOps needs. Remember that it is impossible to create an infallible system. The key is learning to adapt, and this guide brings you one step closer to that, ensuring you always have a solution to any CodeStar connection management problem that comes your way.

6.6. Conclusion

So there you have it—the crux of our deep dive into successfully establishing an efficient connection in AWS CodeStar. We've peeled back the mystique to deliver a practical, hands-on approach designed for both Novice and Pro developers. Draw on these insights, build your connections with skill and precision, and watch your productivity soar!

Chapter 7. The Role of Network Configuration in Connection Stability

Now, let's dive into the intricacies of how network configuration has such a significant role in connection stability. Any seasoned cloud architect will tell you that a proper network configuration is the backbone of any stable, reliable, and secure connection.

7.1. Understanding Network Configuration

Ever wondered how different cloud elements communicate with each other, or how they connect to the internet? Well, that's network configuration for you - a critical, yet often underestimated aspect of AWS CodeStar connection management. An astute understanding and management of the elements that govern your network connectivity - be it public and private subnets, routing tables, or internet gateways - is indispensable to establish a highly functional, stable, and secure connection.

To start with, it's important to understand that AWS CodeStar establishes connections between resources spread across various AWS and third-party services. These services invariably depend on a well-configured network to communicate effectively.

7.2. The Network Blueprint

The backbone of any secured and stable network lies in its architecture - the fundamental blueprint that portrays the 'big picture' of your network configuration. This blueprint comprises of several key elements such as Virtual Private Clouds (VPCs), Subnets, Internet Gateways, and Routing Tables, each playing a crucial role in forging and maintaining connections.

In a nutshell, VPCs provide the sandbox environment where your services exist, subnets divide your VPCs into manageable, isolated chunks, gateways bridge your local network with AWS, and routing tables define the rules of traffic flow.

Balance and interconnectivity between these elements is quintessential. A misconfiguration or imbalance can result in network partitions, potential security threats, service disruption, and ultimately - connectivity woes.

7.3. Getting the VPCs Right

Every connection in AWS starts with a Virtual Private Cloud (VPC). A VPC is essentially a private, isolated part of AWS where you can launch resources in a virtual network that you manage. This allows you to control your environment, including the selection of your IP address range, creation of subnets, and configuration of route tables and network gateways.

By default, your resources within a VPC can communicate with each other. However, enabling the resources of your VPC to communicate with the internet or other services requires diligent configuration - getting it right is crucial for connection stability.

One key caveat here - while creating a VPC is quite simple, avoiding overly complex network layouts could be beneficial. It's all about keeping things minimal while ensuring maximum stability and security.

7.4. Finessing Subnets

Subnets play an integral role in partitioning your network into one or more networks and controlling traffic between them. There are two types of subnets, Public and Private, and the differences are essential to keep in mind for optimal network configuration.

A public subnet is one where instances have direct access to the internet, while a private subnet is where instances do not have direct access. Instead, they can connect to the internet through a Network Address Translation (NAT) gateway residing in the public subnet.

Understanding how, when, and where to partition your network not only bolsters your network's security but also massively augments network stability and communication efficiency.

7.5. Deciphering Routing Tables and Internet Gateways

Routing tables are like the roadmaps of your network, defining how traffic flows between subnets. Every table consists of a set of rules, aptly known as routes, which dictate the allowed traffic paths.

Moreover, to connect your VPC to the internet, an Internet Gateway is needed. It's a 'dual' door that allows inbound and outbound communication to the internet from your VPC. Only those subnets whose route table points to the Internet Gateway can access the internet - and so the circle is closed.

So, there you have it. Network configuration might seem like a daunting aspect of AWS CodeStar, especially given its significant influence on connection stability. But with a firm grasp on the orchestration of VPCs, subnets, routing tables, and Internet Gateways, you're now better positioned to configure an effective, stable, and secure network - which ultimately leads to seamless, problem-free connections across your CodeStar projects.

Towards the end, it's crucial to remember that a well-structured and stable network, just like any tool, is no silver bullet. It takes constant learning, monitoring, and tinkering to keep it at its peak performance.

Remember, the devil lies in the detail. Your active understanding, diligent planning, and proactive management of your network configuration can make your AWS CodeStar connection management issues vanish into thin air.

Chapter 8. Diagnosing and Fixing Connection Woes

In the realm of AWS CodeStar, connection issues often present the first steep climb for developers - a daunting terrain that can intimidate veterans and newcomers alike. That's why we're launching directly into the diagnosing and fixing of 'Connection Woes'.

But, before moving forward, it's vital to understand that difficulty in maintaining connection generally indicates a problem with the underlying infrastructure, poorly configured settings, or inaccessible resources. What follows is a deep dive into these issues and how to resolve them.

8.1. Understanding Connection Flow

To troubleshoot effectively, it's essential to understand how connections are established in CodeStar. The process typically unfolds in three steps:

1. The client creates a connection request to the CodeStar service.

2. CodeStar validates this request and checks the client's permissions.

3. If validated, a connection is established; if not, the connection is denied, and an error message is produced.

Knowing this flow aids in diagnosing where the problem might be originating from, and defining the requisite action to resolve it.

8.2. Diagnosing Connection Problems

Identifying the origin of a connection problem is almost half the battle won. AWS CodeStar provides Error Messages and Log Files that can be extensively used for diagnoses. It's like having a friendly guide showing you where you've stumbled.

8.2.1. Error Messages

Error messages are the immediate response you get when a connection fails. These messages typically include a reason for denial, which can offer an immediate resolution strategy. For instance, an Access Denied error suggests a permissions issue, which can be rectified by adjusting policy settings.

Here's a list of common error messages and what they mean:

- Access Denied: Insufficient permissions.

- Resource Not Found: Requested resources might have been deleted, are unavailable, or the name is misspelled.

- Invalid Request: Improper request structure, or wrong API endpoint was used.

8.2.2. Log Files

Log files are a treasure trove of detailed information and can provide insights into what's going wrong under the hood. To leverage them effectively, ensure proper debugging level is set in logging configuration.

8.3. Fixing Connection Problems

Rediscovering serenity amidst the chaos of connection issues is no longer a pipe dream with the following pointers.

8.3.1. Adjusting User Permissions

If the error message indicated a permissions issue, the fix could be as simple as adjusting your policy settings. Ensure that the IAM user has sufficient permissions to perform the requested operation. It might also help to check that the client has the appropriate roles assigned.

8.3.2. Verifying Resource Availability

If a resource error occurred, validate that the requested resources are available and accessible. This includes checking resource names and spelling, as small typos can result in connection mishaps.

8.3.3. Correcting Request Structure

For `Invalid Request` errors, check the API documentation for the correct request structure. Ensure that the correct HTTP verb (GET, POST, DELETE, etc.) is used, and that all required parameters are provided.

8.4. The Ping Test

The `ping` command can be a valuable tool for identifying network-level connectivity issues. Running a `ping` to the CodeStar server will help determine if the client's network is capable of reaching the server and how much time it takes to get a response. If the `ping` does not succeed, you might need to look into network settings and firewall rules.

8.5. Securing Your Connection

As developers, we need to maintain robust security while ensuring uninterrupted connectivity. SSL/TLS can be used for secure connections in CodeStar. Check for proper SSL configuration, and that your AWS SDK and devices trust the CodeStar certificate authority.

In a nutshell, AWS CodeStar Connection Management primarily requires an analytical mindset to interpret perceived issues correctly, an eye for detail to identify error clues swiftly, and an unwavering resolve to implement solution-driven actions. Armed with these insights, a connectivity issue could become less of a stumbling block and more of an opportunity for in-depth understanding and, ultimately, application success.

Chapter 9. Productive Troubleshooting Tools and Techniques

Before we get into the gritty details of troubleshooting connectivity issues, it's crucial to understand what AWS CodeStar is. Simply put, it's a cloud-based service provided by Amazon Web Services (AWS) for developing, building, and deploying applications on AWS. It integrates with both AWS and third-party tools, allowing developers to manage the lifecycle of their applications within a single platform.

Let's now delve deeper into the world of productive troubleshooting of CodeStar by familiarizing ourselves with various tools and techniques.

9.1. Understanding Comprehensively

Knowledge is power. A comprehensive understanding of how AWS CodeStar operates will take you a long way in resolving connectivity issues. CodeStar utilizes AWS CloudFormation under the hood - so understanding the latter can wield significant influence over your troubleshooting efficacy.

CloudFormation employs a template driven model for infrastructure management, allowing you to describe and provision all the infrastructure resources within your AWS environment. When there is a bit of trouble connecting your source repository with your other AWS Services, have a look at the CloudFormation templates. Examining the template would immediately point you at the right direction where something might have gone haywire.

9.2. Using the AWS Management Console

One of the most efficient ways of dealing with issues you may be facing with CodeStar is to leverage the power of the AWS Management Console. This interface allows you to access and manage Amazon Web Services through a simple and intuitive web-based user interface.

Check your CloudFormation stack through the AWS Management Console. Look for the one created by CodeStar when you established the project. Navigate to the 'Events' section – which would list any errors encountered during the life cycle of your stack. AWS Management Console can present a treasure trove of information and insights for your troubleshooting expedition.

9.3. AWS CLI and SDKs

For those who prefer the command line interface or need programmatic access, AWS provides the AWS Command Line Interface (CLI) and Software Development Kits (SDKs) for different programming languages.

You may use AWS CLI or SDKs to automate checking your CloudFormation stack or performing other debugging actions, saving you time and efficiency in finding issues and solutions.

For instance, using AWS CLI, you can describe stack events to get a detailed overview of all the AWS CloudFormation stack operations. This way, you may reach the root cause of any issue quicker than you might expect.

9.4. Using AWS CloudWatch

AWS Cloudwatch is an incredible tool for monitoring your AWS resources and the applications in real time. By using Cloudwatch, you can collect and track metrics, collect and monitor log files, set alarms, and react to changes in your AWS resources dynamically.

It's a good practice to send your application logs to CloudWatch where you can monitor them for specific text patterns or metrics. If there are any consistency-specific or exception-related issues, CloudWatch logs will be the first place to look into across your implementation.

9.5. Integrating with AWS X-Ray

AWS X-Ray, a service that captures and visualizes requests made by your application, is also a noteworthy troubleshooting technique when debugging and analyzing your applications. X-Ray's trace data provides insights to help you understand how requests travel through your application and where bottlenecks and potential issues are emerging, giving you the agency to resolve connectivity issues better.

9.6. Expert Tip: AWS Trusted Advisor

AWS Trusted Advisor is designed to provide you with a real time guide as per AWS best practices. The 'Service Limits' check can be particularly helpful in the context of connection troubles. If your AWS service is hitting a limit, it can cause issues ranging from throttling to complete connectivity failures. Be sure to check your Service Limits regularly for keeping connection trouble at bay.

Investing work in productive troubleshooting tools and techniques will reward you tenfold in your developer journey of AWS CodeStar. By using the tools perfectly crafted by AWS and combining them with a keen sense of understanding and discretion, you can convert potential crisis into learning opportunities. After all, growth largely stems from how well we navigate our difficulties, and troubleshooting gives you plenty of those to learn from. Happy debugging!

Chapter 10. Best Practices in CodeStar Connection Management

The intricacies of CodeStar connection management may seem like formidable obstacles, but armed with some best practice strategies, you can overcome these hurdles effortlessly, turning upon a steep learning curve with confidence.

10.1. Understanding Connection Management

CodeStar connection management forms an integral part of the AWS developer experience. Facilitating a seamless link between your AWS resources and third-party code repositories like GitHub, GitLab, or Bitbucket, CodeStar Connections may simplify async coding and enhance DevOps practices. However, strategically managing these connections is an art, backed by a clear understanding of their functioning.

1. Understand Project Connection: Every CodeStar project needs a connection to link to your source code, irrespective of the AWS CodePipeline stages.

2. Define Connection Scope: When you create a connection, you define its scope to a particular third-party provider. This connection remains available for AWS services for that defined provider, rendering a connection mobile, able to be used across pipelines.

3. Differentiate CodeStar Connections and GitHub Apps: While both can connect your AWS services to Github, Github Apps require access to all repositories, unlike CodeStar Connections that can

limit access to chosen repositories.

10.2. Setting Up CodeStar Connections

Having understood their significance, let's discuss the established practices to set up CodeStar Connections:

1. Ensure Permissions: Start the connection process with the right permissions. Create an IAM policy that allows 'codestar-connections:UseConnection'. This policy will enable pipeline tasks to use the connection.

2. Initiate the Connection: Create a connection in the AWS Management Console under the Developer Tools category. Choose the provider type and follow the step-by-step wizards to establish the connection.

3. Install the App: During the above step, you will be redirected to install the AWS Connector for your chosen provider. Ensure the app has the correct permissions for seamless operation.

4. Confirm the Connection: After installation, return to AWS Management Console and select the newly created connection, ensuring the status turns to 'Available'.

10.3. Implementing Connection Security

A critical factor to keep in mind is connection security. Mismanaged connections could lead to security issues, making your code vulnerable.

1. Limit Repository Access: Carefully choose the repositories you give access to while installing the AWS Connector app on your

third-party provider. Specificity ensures better security.

2. Handle Webhook Events: The AWS Connector app needs rights to read repository metadata and handle webhook events carefully. Mismanaged webhooks could invite unwanted security risks.

3. Manage IAM Policies: Connections have a broad reach and can be used by any AWS service that interacts with third-party providers. Assign explicit permissions in IAM policies to limit this scope to necessary interactions only.

10.4. Troubleshooting Connection Issues

Despite following best practices, you may encounter hiccups in the process. Understanding how to troubleshoot these issues is key to a smooth DevOps experience.

1. Check Connection Status: Firstly, ensure your connection's status is 'Available'. An 'Unavailable' or 'Pending' status may indicate an issue requiring attention.

2. Validate AWS Connector App Permissions: If your connection status is fine, but you are still experiencing problems, verify the permissions given to the AWS Connector app. Ensure the app can read repository metadata and handle webhooks.

3. Use CloudWatch: AWS CloudWatch can provide logs for pipeline stages. Monitoring these logs can give insight into potential issues, helping trace the root cause of the problem.

Incorporating these practices in your daily DevOps tasks can profoundly impact your CodeStar connection management efficiency. Developing a strong understanding and keen awareness of potential pitfalls will equip you to make the most out of your AWS projects, streamlining your cloud development experience. Always remember, every obstacle is an opportunity for progress; every connection issue, a lesson in the art of troubleshooting. With persistence and the right toolkit, you are well on your to mastering CodeStar Connection Management.

Chapter 11. Looking Ahead: The Future of CodeStar and Connection Management

While the journey of advancing through the present intricacies of AWS CodeStar holds its fair share of challenges, an exciting fact that we can't overlook is the promising future that lies ahead. As of now, AWS CodeStar, like any other brilliant software development tool, is continually evolving. Let's dive deep into some of the anticipated developments in the realm of AWS CodeStar and its connection management landscape.

11.1. The Advent of Automated Connection Management

One of the significant future trends that we foresee in CodeStar revolves around automated connection management. With the soaring demands for efficient and intuitive DevOps practices, streamlined connectivity is no longer a luxury but a necessity. Automated connection management will likely reduce the workload of developers significantly, granted that the manual effort needed to establish, maintain, and troubleshoot connections will be culled down substantially.

This automation won't just stop at the formation of connections; we are foreseeing continuous monitoring and self-healing features being integrated. This automated vigilance coupled with self-correction will react proactively to any disruptions occurring within the connections, restoring them swiftly with minimized downtime.

11.2. The Role of AI in Connection Management

Another potentially transformational concept in the pipeline for CodeStar's future roadmap is the incorporation of Artificial Intelligence. While AI-powered solutions have already been pervading various aspects of technology, they will prove revolutionary when brought into connection management.

AI could help with predictive analytics, pointing out potential issues before they escalate into bigger problems. Not only that, it can also learn from previous errors and prevent similar connection issues from recurring in the future. The inclusion of AI in connection management might sound far-fetched, but given the fast-paced advancements in tech, it might be closer to realization than we think.

11.3. Enhancing the User Experience with Interactive Interfaces

A well-engineered connection manager is critical to the proper functioning of CodeStar. However, the potential addition of a more interactive, user-friendly GUI could allow developers to visualize and manipulate connections in a much more intuitive manner. This modernized interface will pave the way for greater developer engagement and error-free connection management.

11.4. Fortifying Security in Connection Management

Security breaches are a dreaded scenario for any tech product, and connection management is no exception. As connection management evolves, we also foresee bolstered security protocols and advanced encryption techniques. These upgrades will ensure the data transmission remains secure, making CodeStar a more trustworthy platform to rely on.

11.5. Integration with More AWS Services

As AWS continues its mission to deploy more specialized services, we can expect CodeStar to work seamlessly with these new additions. The future of CodeStar connection management holds the promise of versatile integrations, providing developers with a more unified and expansive cloud environment.

11.6. Conclusion

There's no denying that the future of AWS CodeStar and its connection management appears bright and full of potential. The mentioned developments are just our educated projections based on current trends and indications. The actual future might even surpass these predictions as technology continually springs surprises. For developers, understanding these potential changes and staying updated is paramount to navigating this ever-evolving landscape successfully.

Indeed, there will be more challenges as CodeStar continues to evolve. However, remember - every hurdle can be a stepping stone to greater knowledge. Let us embrace the coming changes with open minds and adaptive strategies, turning these future challenges into learning opportunities.

While specifics about the route CodeStar will take remain hazy, one thing is clear: AWS CodeStar, with its connection management component, is on a set path to transform how we undertake software development and deployment. Tuning in to these potential developments and growing alongside them could be a great leap forward for both developers and organizations alike.